CHRISTMAS PIANO SOLOS

Book: ISBN 978-1-4234-5690-2

Book/CD: ISBN 978-1-4234-5695-7

WILLIS MUSIC

Exclusively Distributed By

HAL•LEONARD®
CORPORATION
7777 W. BLUEMOUND RD. P.O. BOX 13819 MILWAUKEE, WI 53213

Visit Hal Leonard Online at
www.halleonard.com

Contents

Frosty the Snow Man

Use with John Thompson's Modern Course for the Piano
SECOND GRADE BOOK, after page 6.

Words and Music by Steve Nelson
and Jack Rollins
Arranged by Glenda Austin

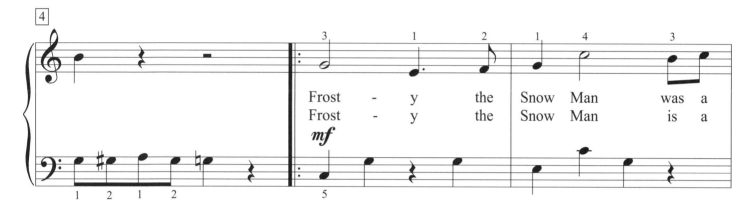

Frost - y   the   Snow Man   was a
Frost - y   the   Snow Man   is a

jol - ly, hap - py   soul   with a   corn - cob pipe   and a
fair - y tale they   say;   he was   made of snow   but the

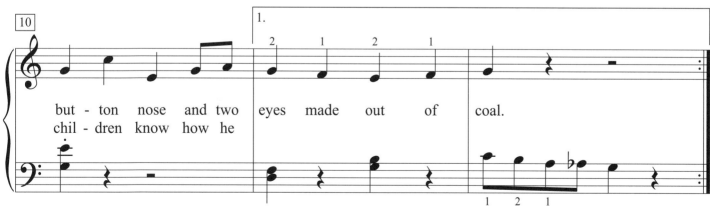

but - ton nose and two   eyes made out of   coal.
chil - dren know how he

came to life one day. There must have been some mag - ic in that

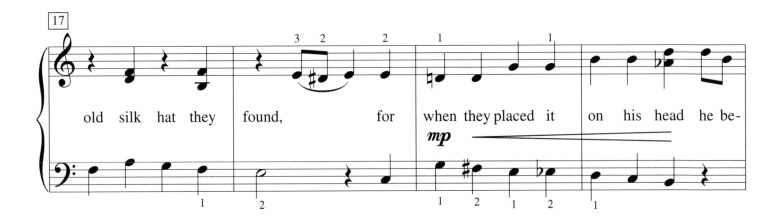

old silk hat they found, for when they placed it on his head he be-

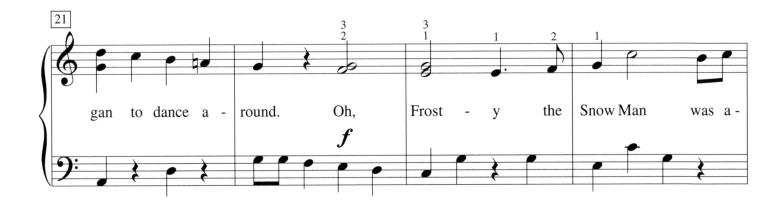

gan to dance a - round. Oh, Frost - y the Snow Man was a-

live as he could be, and the chil-dren say he could laugh and play just the

same as you and me. Thump-et-y thump thump, thump-et-y thump thump,

look at Frost-y go. Thump-et-y thump thump,

thump-et-y thump thump, o-ver the hills of snow.

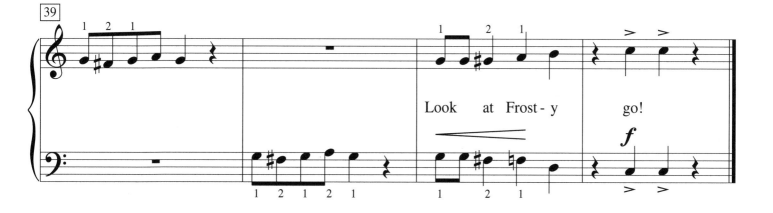

Look at Frost-y go!

Dance of the Sugar Plum Fairy

from THE NUTCRACKER

Use after page 11.

By Pyotr Il'yich Tchaikovsky
Arranged by Glenda Austin

I Heard the Bells on Christmas Day

Use after page 18.

Words by Henry Wadsworth Longfellow
Adapted by Johnny Marks
Music by Johnny Marks
Arranged by Glenda Austin

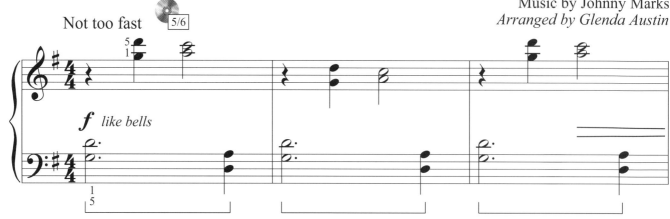

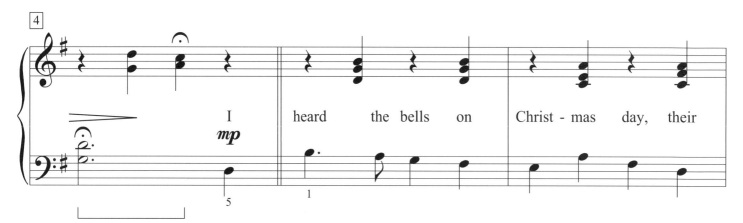

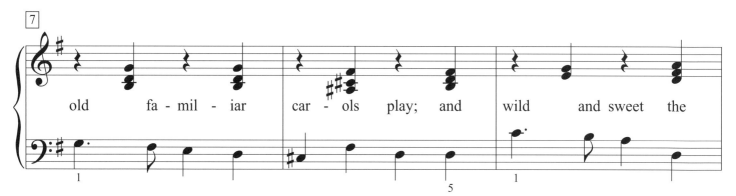

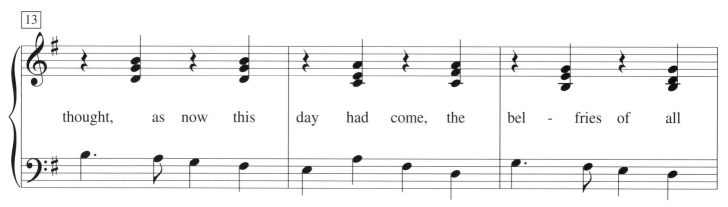

thought, as now this day had come, the bel - fries of all

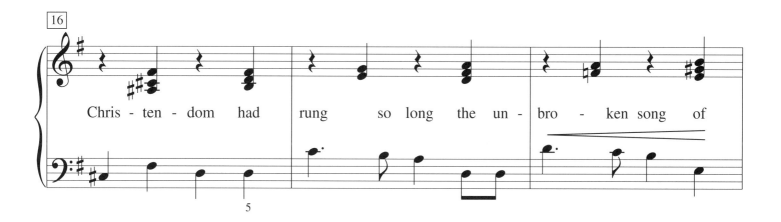

Chris - ten - dom had rung so long the un - bro - ken song of

5

peace on earth, good will to men.

poco rit.

mf

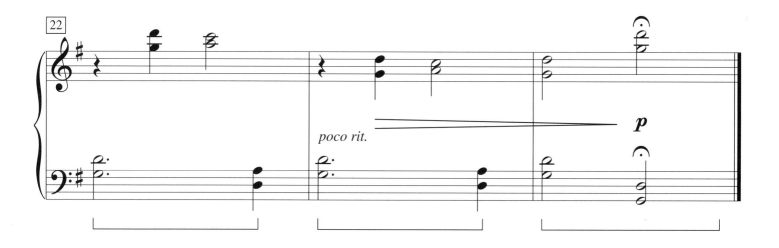

poco rit.

p

I Saw Mommy Kissing Santa Claus

Use after page 23.

Words and Music by Tommie Connor
Arranged by Glenda Austin

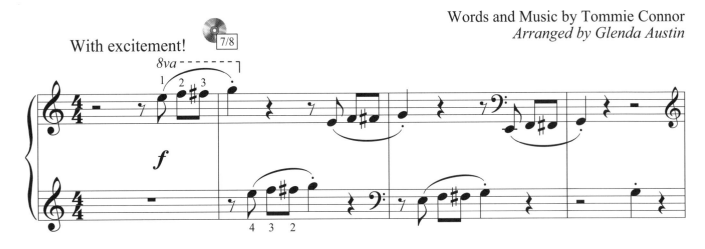

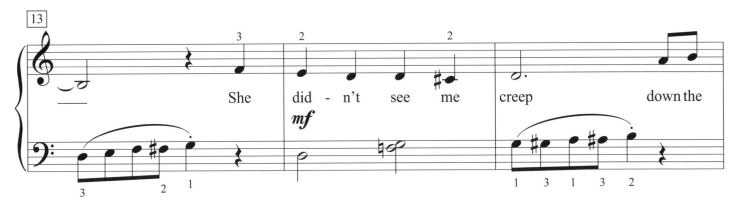

stairs to have a peep, she thought that I was tucked up in my

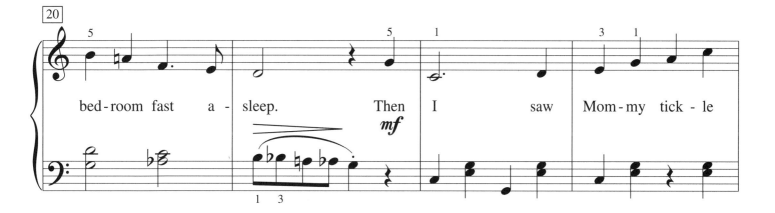

bed-room fast a-sleep. Then I saw Mom-my tick-le

San - ta Claus, un-der-neath his beard so snow-y

white. _____ Oh, what a laugh that would have

been,   if   Dad - dy had   on - ly   seen   Mom - my

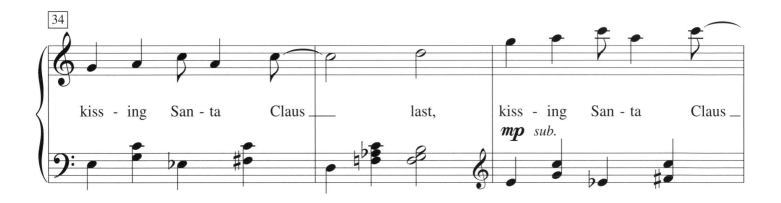

kiss - ing   San - ta   Claus _____   last,   kiss - ing   San - ta   Claus _____

_mp_ _sub._

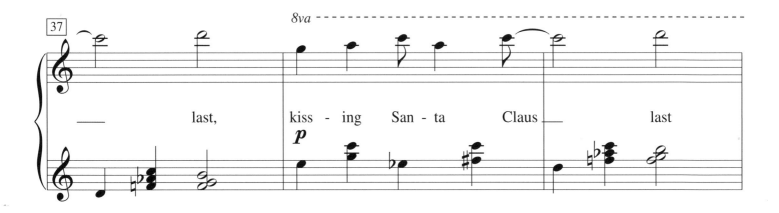

_____   last,   kiss - ing   San - ta   Claus _____   last

_p_

night.

_f_

The Chipmunk Song

Use after page 28.

Words and Music by Ross Bagdasarian
Arranged by Glenda Austin

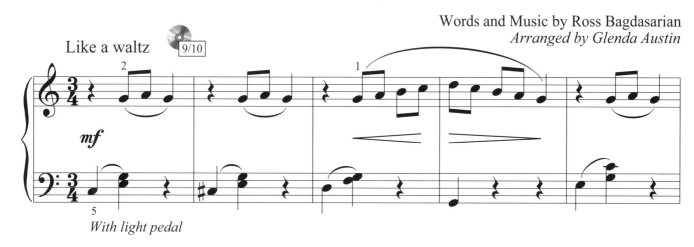

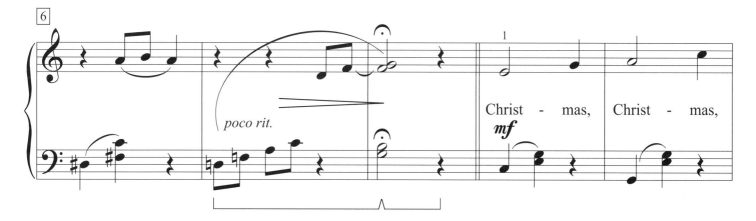

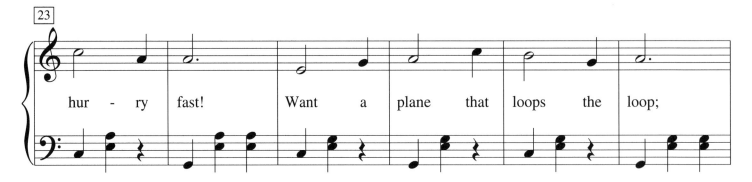

hur - ry fast! Want a plane that loops the loop;

me, I want a hu - la hoop. We can hard - ly

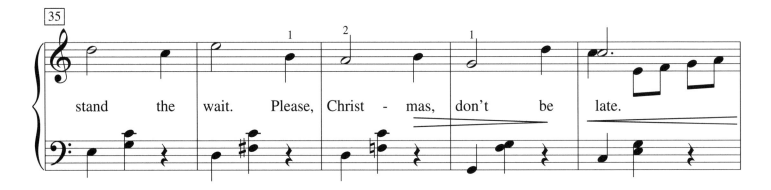

stand the wait. Please, Christ - mas, don't be late.

mf cantabile

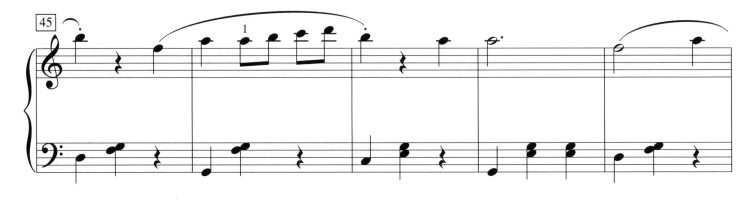

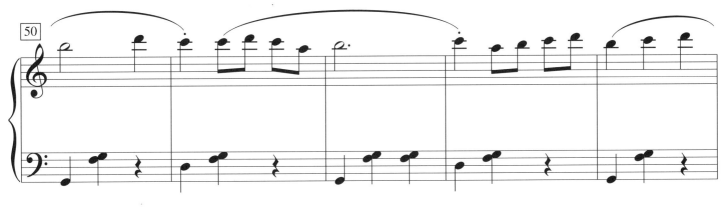

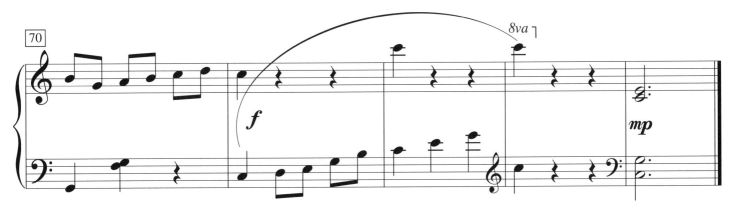

My Favorite Things
from THE SOUND OF MUSIC
Use after page 33.

Lyrics by Oscar Hammerstein II
Music by Richard Rodgers
Arranged by Glenda Austin

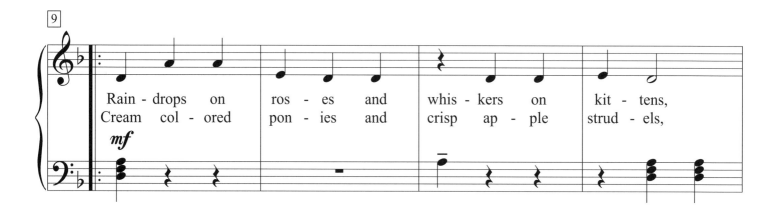

Rain - drops on ros - es and whis - kers on kit - tens,
Cream col - ored pon - ies and crisp ap - ple strud - els,

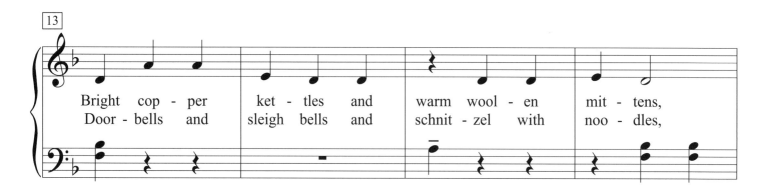

Bright cop - per ket - tles and warm wool - en mit - tens,
Door - bells and sleigh bells and schnit - zel with noo - dles,

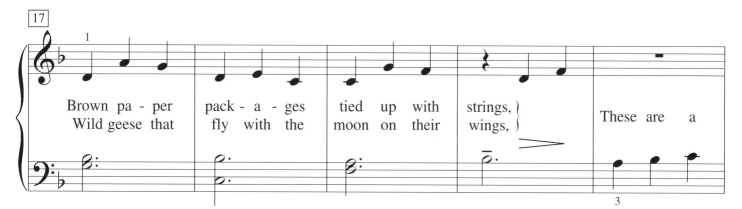

Brown pa - per / Wild geese that pack - a - ges / fly with the tied up with / moon on their strings, / wings, These are a

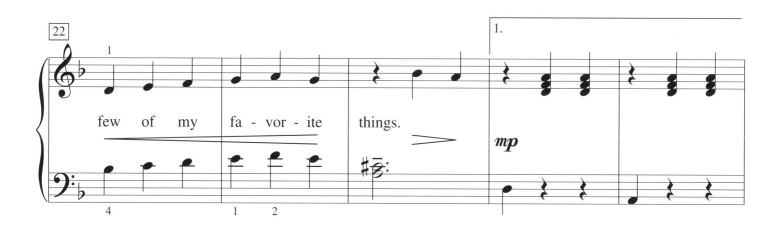

few of my fa - vor - ite things. *mp*

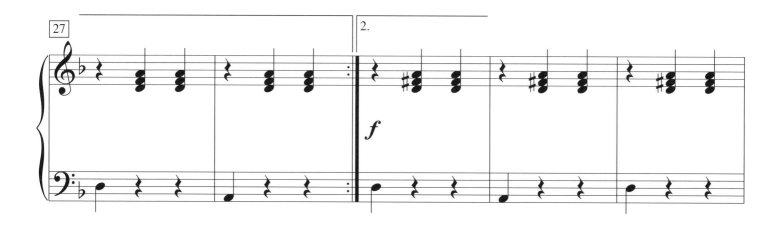

f

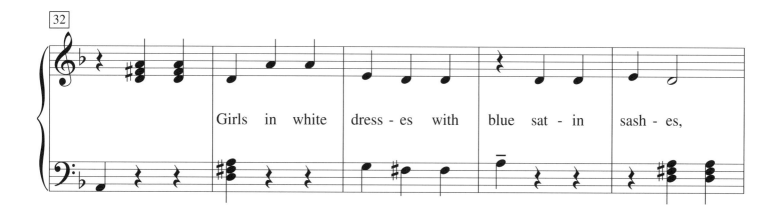

Girls in white dress - es with blue sat - in sash - es,

Snow-flakes that stay on my nose and eye - lash - es, Sil - ver white

win - ters that melt in - to springs, These are a few of my

fa - vor - ite things. When the dog bites,

poco rit.

f *a tempo*

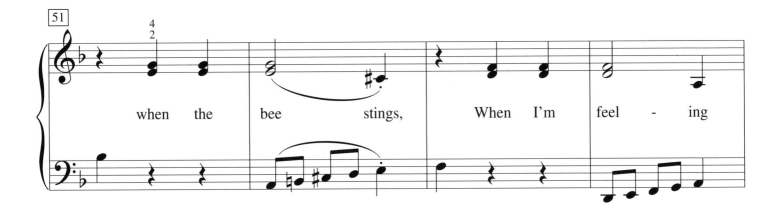

when the bee stings, When I'm feel - ing

sad, I sim - ply re - mem - ber my

fa - vor - ite things and then I don't feel

broaden so bad. *a tempo*

Let It Snow! Let It Snow! Let It Snow!

Use after page 39.

Words by Sammy Cahn
Music by Jule Styne
Arranged by Glenda Austin

With a bounce

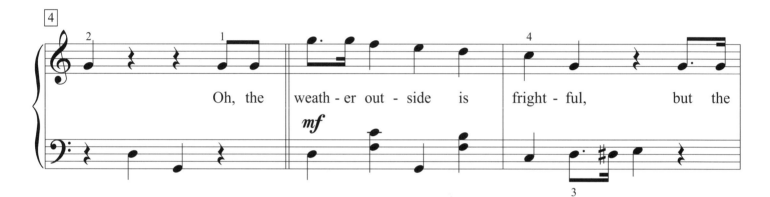

Oh, the weath-er out-side is fright-ful, but the

fire is so de-light-ful, and since we've no place to

go, Let it snow! Let it snow! Let it snow! It

does - n't show signs of stop - ping, and I brought some corn for

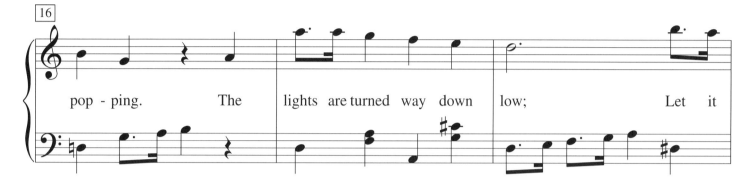

pop - ping. The lights are turned way down low; Let it

snow! Let it snow! Let it snow! When we fi - nal - ly kiss good -

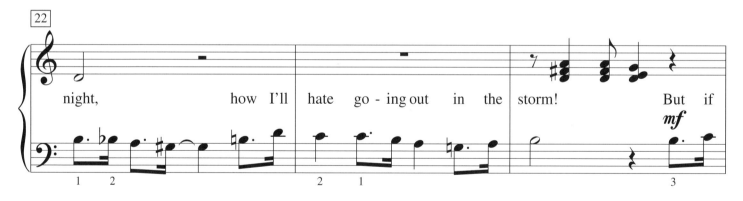

night, how I'll hate go - ing out in the storm! But if

you'll real - ly hold me tight, all the way home I'll be

warm.   The   fi - re is slow - ly   dy - ing   and, my

dear,   we're still   good - bye - ing,   but as long as you love me

so,   Let it snow! Let it snow! Let it snow!

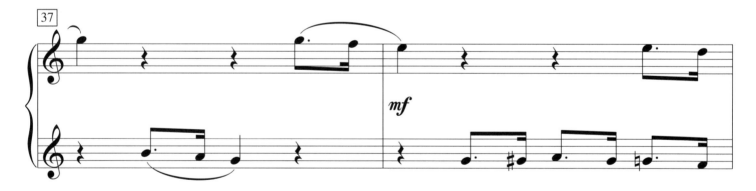

poco rit.

Jingle, Jingle, Jingle

Use after page 51.

Music and Lyrics by Johnny Marks
Arranged by Glenda Austin

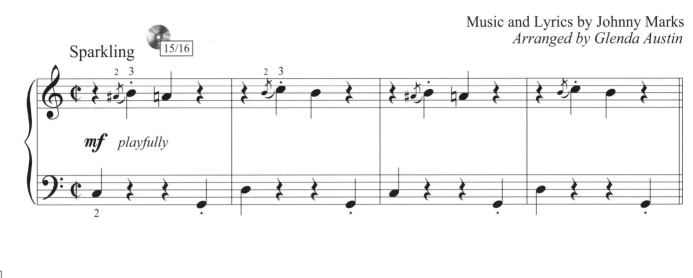

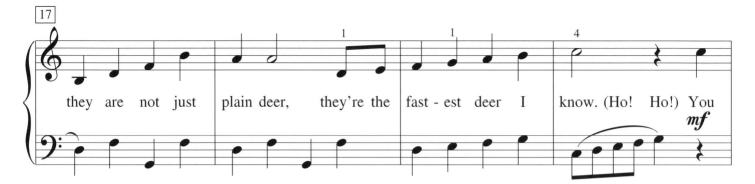

they are not just plain deer, they're the fast-est deer I know. (Ho! Ho!) You

must be-lieve that on Christ-mas Eve I won't pass you by. I'll

dash a-way in my mag-ic sleigh, fly-ing through the sky.

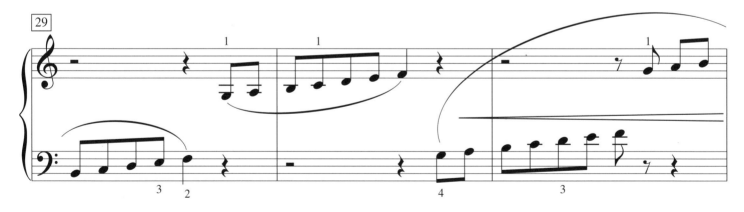

Jin - gle, jin - gle, jin - gle, you will

hear my sleigh bells ring, I am old Kris

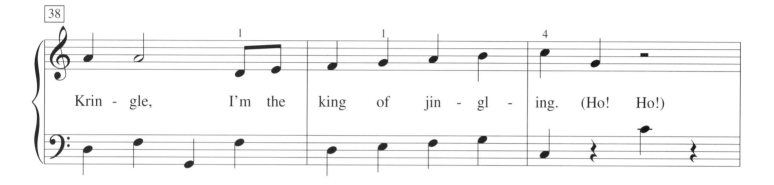

Krin - gle, I'm the king of jin - gl - ing. (Ho! Ho!)

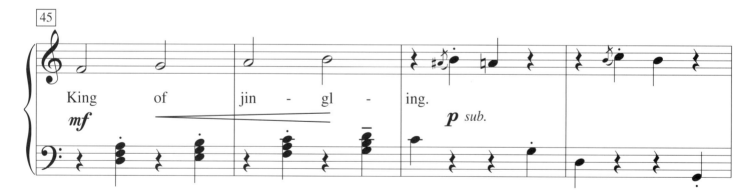

King of jin - gl - ing.

Christmas Is

Use after page 65.

Lyrics by Spence Maxwell
Music by Percy Faith
Arranged by Glenda Austin

just can't __ go to sleep; Christ-mas is mem-'ries, the

kind you __ al-ways keep. Deck the halls and __ give a

cheer for all the things that Christ-mas is each year.

Christ-mas, __ Mer-ry Christ-mas, __ when

all your wish-es come true.   Christ-mas is car-ols to

warm you ___ in the snow;   Christ-mas is bed - time where

no one ___ wants to go.   All the world is ___ tin - sel

bright,   so glad to know that Christ-mas is to - night. _____

Christ-mas, _ Mer-ry Christ-mas, _ when all your wish-es come

true. Christ-mas, _ Mer-ry Christ-mas, _ may

poco rit.

all your wish - es come true.

a tempo

rit.

Because It's Christmas

(For All the Children)

Use after page 75.

Music by Barry Manilow
Lyric by Bruce Sussman and Jack Feldman
Arranged by Glenda Austin

To - night the stars shine   for the   chil - dren, _____
To - night be - longs to   all the   chil - dren. _____

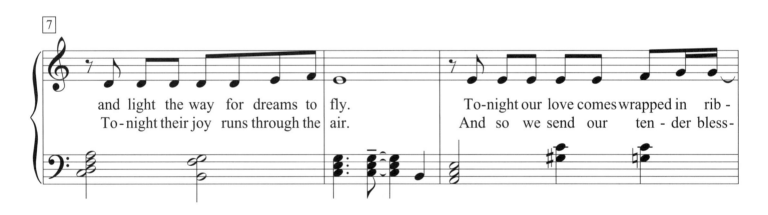

and light the way for dreams to | fly.   To-night our love comes wrapped in   rib -
To-night their joy runs through the | air.   And so we send our   ten - der bless-

- bons. _   The world is right and hopes are | high.
- ings _   to all the chil - dren ev -'ry- | where.

13

And from a dark _ and frost-ed | win - dow _ a child _ ap-|pears _ to search _ the
To see the smiles _and hear the | laugh - ter, a time _ to | give, a time _ to

16 | **1.**

sky be - cause _ it's | Christ - mas, be - cause it's | Christ - mas.
share, be - cause _ it's | | *poco rit.*

19 | **2.**

Christ - mas for now _ and for -|ev - er for all _ of the | chil - dren and for the

22

chil - dren in us | all. | |
poco rit. | *a tempo* | *poco rit.* | *pp*

A DOZEN A DAY

by Edna Mae Burnam

The **Dozen a Day** books are universally recognized as one of the most remarkable technique series on the market for all ages! Each book in this series contains short warm-up exercises to be played at the beginning of each practice session, providing excellent day-to-day training for the student. The audio CD is playable on any CD player and features fabulous backing tracks by Ric Iannone. For Windows® and Mac computer users, the CD is enhanced so you can access MIDI files for each exercise and adjust the tempo.

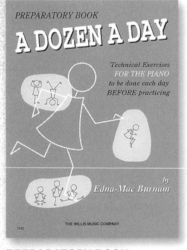

PREPARATORY BOOK
00414222	Book Only	$3.95
00406476	Book/CD Pack	$8.95
00406479	CD Only	$9.95
00406477	Book/GM Disk Pack	$13.95
00406480	GM Disk Only	$9.95

BOOK 1
00413366	Book Only	$3.95
00406481	Book/CD Pack	$8.95
00406483	CD Only	$9.95
00406482	Book/GM Disk Pack	$13.90
00406484	GM Disk Only	$9.95

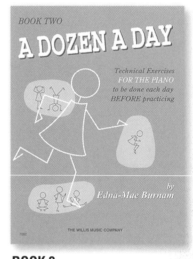

BOOK 2
00413826	Book Only	$3.95
00406485	Book/CD Pack	$8.95
00406487	CD Only	$9.95
00406486	Book/GM Disk Pack	$13.90
00406488	GM Disk Only	$9.95

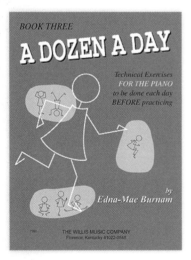

BOOK 3
00414136	Book Only	$4.95
00416760	Book/CD Pack	$9.95

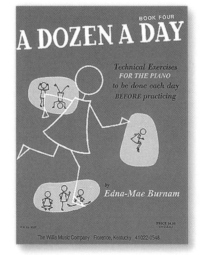

BOOK 4
00415686	Book Only	$5.95
00416761	Book/CD Pack	$10.95

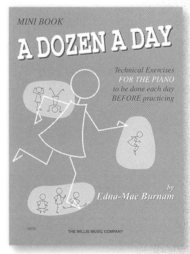

MINI BOOK
00404073	Mini Book	$3.95
00406472	Book/CD Pack	$8.95
00406474	CD Only	$9.95
00406473	Book/GM Disk Pack	$13.90
00406475	GM Disk Only	$9.95

WILLIS MUSIC

EXCLUSIVELY DISTRIBUTED BY
HAL•LEONARD®

Prices, contents, and availability subject to change without notice. Prices listed in U.S. funds.